RED CROSS
Red Crescent

▲▲▲▲▲▲▲▲▲▲▲▲▲▲

When Help
CAN'T WAIT

DISCARD

LESLIE BURGER

DEBRA L. RAHM

LERNER PUBLICATIONS COMPANY
MINNEAPOLIS

Library of Congress Cataloging-in-Publication Data

Burger, Leslie.
    Red Cross/Red Crescent: when help can't wait/by Leslie Burger and Debra L. Rahm.
        p.   cm.—(International cooperation series)
    Includes index.
    Summary: Provides a history of the Red Cross and discusses the philosophy and work of the societies that are part of this international organization.
    ISBN 0-8225-2698-0 (alk. paper)
    1. Red Cross—Juvenile literature. 2. Red Cross—History—Juvenile Literature. [1. Red Cross—History.] I. Rahm, Debra L. II. Title.

HV568.B87 1996
361.7'7—dc20
                                                                    96-384

Manufactured in the United States of America
1 2 3 4 5 6 – JR – 01 00 99 98 97 96

CONTENTS

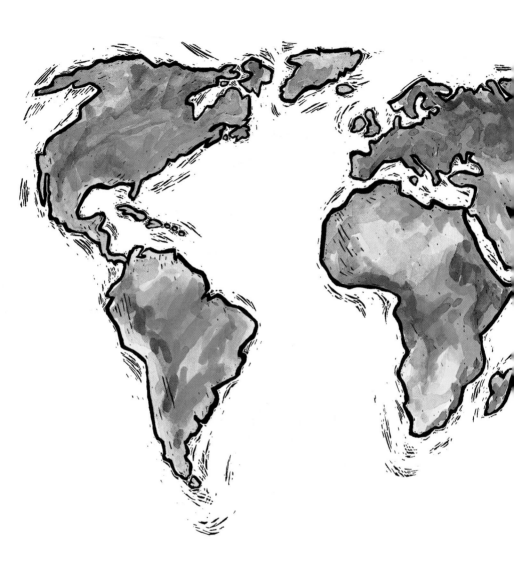

Help Is Here

Day was breaking in the central Asian city of Kabul, the capital of Afghanistan. A small group arrived at the city's prison, where antigovernment rebel fighters were being held as prisoners of war (POWs). The visitors were delegates, or representatives, of the **International Committee of the Red Cross (ICRC).** They had come to give the prisoners messages from their families. Some of the prisoners had been waiting for months to receive word from their loved ones.

When the delegates entered the prison compound, "the news of our arrival spread like wildfire," one of the delegates reported. "Soon a crowd began to gather. The prisoners, eager to receive their messages, pressed closer."

The prisoners passed around the photographs they'd received from home and openly shared their precious letters with their cellmates. Usually, letters "are read aloud and freely commented on by everyone in the cell," said the delegate.

Some of the prisoners wrote letters in response. Several weeks later, the delegate explained, the ICRC would deliver the letters to the prisoners' families—one of many services it provides to POWs.

In April 1991, a cyclone devastated Bangladesh, a nation in southern Asia. Hardest hit was the country's southern coast, which faces the Bay of Bengal. The cyclone caused tidal waves to surge inland, threatening the lives of the seven million Bangladeshis in the region. The flooding swamped countless fields and killed at least a million cattle.

In addition, an estimated 140,000 people died. Their bodies quickly began to decompose. In some areas, reported one observer, the streams were "black from decomposing corpses," which contaminated the water and posed a serious risk of disease to survivors.

Within a week, the **International Federation of Red Cross and Red Crescent Societies** had mobilized thousands of volunteers from many countries. The volunteers began to bury the mountains of corpses—risking their own lives in the process.

On April 19, 1995, a bomb exploded at the Alfred P. Murrah Federal Building in Oklahoma City, Oklahoma. The huge blast instantly demolished the building, killed 169 people, and injured another 830.

Within minutes of the explosion, the Oklahoma County chapter of the **American Red Cross** was on the scene.

After a cyclone in Bangladesh (*left*), Red Cross/Red Crescent workers quickly brought aid. Michelle Walley comforted one victim of the Oklahoma City bombing (*right*).

One of the volunteers was 19-year-old Michelle Walley. As soon as she heard about the disaster, Walley headed downtown. "When I arrived," she said, "people were . . . trying to get people out of the building and help all the injured people as they came out." Then came a bomb scare—a threat of another explosion. "Everyone had to leave the area," said Walley. "It was very difficult to leave the injured people still inside the building."

As soon as the immediate rescue phase was over, Walley and other Red Cross workers began to supply meals to rescue workers and family members of victims (in all, 3,000 American Red Cross workers supplied 37,000 meals in the first week after the disaster). Eventually, 9,500 American Red Cross workers were on the scene, providing not only meals but also transportation,

Emblems of Aid

The emblem of the International Committee of the Red Cross is a red cross on a white background. Many national societies also use the red cross. In many Muslim countries, however, national societies use a red crescent. That's because many Muslims viewed the cross as a symbol of Christianity. The International Federation of Red Cross and Red Crescent Societies uses both the red cross and red crescent. A third emblem, a red Star of David, is used in Israel.

The emblems are recognized everywhere as symbols of neutral aid. They were created to identify Red Cross and Red Crescent—or military medical—buildings, workers, vehicles, and supplies. Use of the emblems for any other purpose is forbidden.

crisis counseling, shelter, travel and burial expenses, and other services.

Three Branches of a Global Effort

The messengers in Afghanistan, the volunteers in Bangladesh, the rescue workers in Oklahoma in the United States—all are part of the international Red Cross and Red Crescent movement, a global effort dedicated to helping people in times of need. To people around the world, the Red Cross and Red Crescent emblems mean "Help Is Here."

A Red Cross delegate may be the only person who will believe what a prisoner of war says about conditions in the prison. For a survivor in a war-ravaged land, a truck bearing the well-known red cross on a white background may bring vital, clean drinking water. For the victim of a flood, Red Crescent workers may be the only source of a warm blanket and a lifesaving bowl of rice.

The Red Cross and Red Crescent movement consists of three branches. Two international organizations work around the world. A third branch is made up of many organizations that work on a national level, within their own countries.

The ICRC

One of the movement's international organizations is the International Committee of the Red Cross. The ICRC helps victims of armed conflict. In 1994, about 6,000 ICRC delegates worked in the field—that is, in conflict zones—in about 40 countries.

The ICRC provides medical care to soldiers and to civilians who are victims of war. It also provides relief—daily necessities such as food, shelter, water, and clothing—for them. Its representatives visit prisoners of war. Through its Central Tracing Agency (CTA), it delivers messages that would be difficult to send or receive otherwise. The CTA also reunites family members who have been separated during a crisis.

The ICRC's headquarters are in Geneva, Switzerland. It has offices in over 60 countries. It is not tied to any government, and it is funded entirely by donations.

Although the ICRC works in conflict zones, it never takes sides in a conflict. Instead, it helps victims on all sides. Because the ICRC is neutral, it is often the only organization allowed in a conflict zone.

The Federation

The second international organization is the International Federation of Red Cross and Red Crescent Societies. The Federation assists victims of accidents and natural disasters. Like the ICRC, the Federation supplies relief after an emergency. It asks countries around the world for money, people, and other resources.

The Federation is an alliance of national Red Cross and Red Crescent societies, which are represented in its General Assembly. The Federation does most of its work through the national societies, coordinating their efforts.

But it is also an independent international organization with programs of its own.

Like the ICRC, the Federation's headquarters are in Geneva, Switzerland. Although its headquarters are in Switzerland, it is not part of the Swiss government—or of any government. Often the Federation works with other humanitarian groups to accomplish its tasks.

National Societies

National societies form the third branch of the movement. Nearly every country has a Red Cross or Red Crescent society. In 1995, more than 160 national societies were active. In the United States, the national society is the American Red Cross.

National societies have an important job: to help people in emergencies. But they also sponsor ongoing programs such as blood donation services, first aid and water safety courses, nurse training courses, and youth programs.

Working Together

Although the ICRC, the Federation, and the national societies perform separate duties, they often work together. For example, when the ICRC enters a conflict zone, it often relies on the national societies in the area for workers, equipment, and information.

The three branches of the Red Cross and Red Crescent movement meet once every four years at an international conference. The delegates at the conference consider worldwide problems and decide how to tackle them. They might discuss how to help the growing number of refugees. They might discuss what they can do to help stop the spread of AIDS—the deadly disease caused by the human immunodeficiency virus (HIV).

As the people of the Red Cross/Red Crescent work together, they never forget that their mission is to help people in need. No task is too small. Every hand held, every meal served, every life saved is a victory.

This book will tell you more about the work of the Red Cross/Red Crescent. It will explain how the Red Cross/Red Crescent got started. It will share the stories of people who have received immediate—and dramatic—help in times of crisis. It will explain what Red Cross and Red Crescent volunteers do. And it will show you how you can get involved, if you wish, in work that affects the lives of people in need everywhere.

Chapter One

A Memory and a Dream

ullets and cannonballs exploded wildly in all directions. Sabers clashed and shone with blood. Shrieks of agony filled the air as thousands of soldiers slaughtered one another with every weapon available, even their bare hands. As soldiers and horses fell, troops on both sides advanced, trampling the dead and wounded in their brutal fight.

The Battle of Solferino, fought in 1859, was one of the bloodiest battles of its century. It was a decisive match between the Austrian Empire and its enemy, allied French and Italian forces. At that time, the Austrian Empire covered present-day Austria as well as parts of present-day Italy, Hungary, Poland, the Czech Republic, Slovakia,

Croatia, and Slovenia. France, under the rule of Emperor Napoleon III (the nephew of Napoleon I), had agreed to help Italy defeat the powerful Austrians.

The Battle of Solferino lasted 16 hours and moved through four towns before the Austrians finally fled. When the smoke settled, 40,000 wounded men were left behind. But no medical teams rushed to give them first aid. No ambulances arrived to carry them to hospitals. Instead, the injured men lay on the ground for hours— bleeding, thirsty, and hungry. Many died on the battlefield because no effort was made to save their lives.

Others were gradually brought into nearby villages. Since the villages did not have enough hospitals to care for so many wounded, the injured men were taken to churches and private homes. Once there, they were barely attended to by exhausted volunteers who knew little or nothing about medical care. A man who had watched the battle and its aftermath wrote later, "How many silent tears were shed that miserable night, when all false pride, all human decency even, were forgotten!"

The observer was a chance visitor to Solferino, Swiss businessman Henry Dunant. That night, he took pity on the suffering men. His actions became the basis for the international Red Cross movement.

All Are Brothers

Jean Henri Dunant was born on May 8, 1828, in Geneva, Switzerland. As a youth, he was a poor student; he was more interested in reading books and thinking about food than in completing assigned schoolwork. As a teenager, Henry (as he called himself) was a devout Christian who believed in a life of charity. Once a week he visited the city prison to read to prisoners. During the 1850s, when Henry was in his 20s, he was involved in the establishment of the Young Men's Christian Association (YMCA).

Henry Dunant

Dunant became a banker and later owned businesses in the African country of Algeria, which was ruled by France. Hoping to solve some problems of his businesses there, Dunant decided to speak with Napoleon III. The French emperor was then in northern Italy, leading French troops in the war against the Austrian Empire, so Dunant traveled there. He arrived in Solferino just in time to witness the Battle of Solferino. He wrote, "Things should not be like this. Even if men have to fight, they should be wise enough and civilized enough to pick up the victims and take care of them."

When the battle ended, Dunant acted quickly, using the organizational skills he had developed as a businessman. He arranged for some of the wounded to be brought to a church in Castiglione, a nearby town. He mobilized townspeople to clean and dress wounds, find supplies, and bring fresh water to the patients. Although many of the wounded were enemy soldiers, Dunant persuaded the caregivers to treat all patients equally. "*Tutti fratelli*," he said. "All are brothers."

The Battle of Solferino wounded thousands of soldiers.

Dunant walked among the injured men, giving comfort and what medical care he could. He worked tirelessly, without sleep, for three days. Finally the patients were moved to hospitals in larger cities where their wounds could be treated properly.

The delay of those few days was too much for many of the men, however. Their wounds had become infected during the long hours they had lain on the battlefield. Some of the men died. Dunant agonized over the lack of proper medical care that led to these deaths.

Because of the battle, Dunant never spoke with the

French emperor. For months afterward, he neglected his business affairs. The memory of Solferino would not leave him. He was haunted by visions of that terrible battle and by his belief that so much suffering need not take place.

In 1862 he wrote and published a book about his recollections. A *Memory of Solferino* described the battle itself, the agony afterward, and the efforts of local people to help the wounded. Most important, Dunant included his ideas about how to avoid such needless suffering in the future. "Would it not be possible, in a time of peace and quiet," he asked, "to form relief societies of zealous, devoted, and thoroughly qualified volunteers to bring aid to the wounded in time of war?" Dunant's book outlined a plan that included trained volunteers and well-equipped ambulances. It also suggested a system for delivering messages, keeping records of the dead, and supplying equipment and food.

A Movement Is Born

A *Memory of Solferino* was an immediate and overwhelming success. Dunant had struck a chord in people's hearts about the treatment of wounded soldiers. The year after Dunant's book was published, four prominent Geneva citizens joined Dunant on a committee to put his ideas into practice. At their first meeting, the five men discussed the ideas that later formed the basis of Red Cross action: trained nurses on the battlefield, well-equipped field hospitals, vehicles for transporting the wounded, and a permanent international organization.

Then they invited representatives of other countries to a conference in Geneva to discuss their ideas. Delegates from 16 countries attended the meeting in 1863. The delegates developed the ideas that later became the guiding principles of the Red Cross. Henry Dunant insisted on one of those principles: Medical workers, ambulance drivers, and hospital staff should be considered neutral—not part of a conflict—and so should not be fired upon, taken prisoner, or prevented from giving aid.

At this first conference, delegates chose an emblem to signify neutrality: the red cross on a white background. The symbol is the reverse of the Swiss flag (a white cross on a red background). Switzerland has not been involved in a foreign war for nearly five centuries. The delegates hoped the emblem would remind people of Switzerland's long-standing neutrality.

Henry Dunant promoted the idea of neutrality on a trip he made later that year to create interest in the new Red Cross. As he visited influential people throughout Europe, his intense belief in his cause won him many supporters.

The following year, delegates from 16 nations gathered in Geneva again. Their task this time was to develop permanent rules for the treatment of people wounded in conflicts. They wrote a convention, or treaty, called the Geneva Convention. It set forth, for the first time, international humanitarian laws. The notion of humanitarian law says that every person has the right to be treated with dignity, even in times of armed conflict.

The convention also officially established the emblem of the red cross and outlined rules for its use. On September 1, 1864, most of the attending nations (12 in all) signed the convention. By 1867, 21 nations had signed the convention.

Meanwhile, Henry Dunant, busy with his book and the Red Cross movement, had let his business affairs slide. In 1867, at the height of his triumph with the Red Cross, he went bankrupt. He lost everything—his businesses, his money, his pride. Humiliated, he left Geneva and went to live in Paris. Even though he was now poor, he continued to work for humanitarian causes such as the abolition of slavery and improvement in prison conditions.

The Geneva Convention, later called the First Geneva Convention, was developed at an international conference in 1864.

In Paris, Dunant found himself in the middle of one of the first armed conflicts faced by the newly formed Red Cross. During a war in 1870–1871 between France and Prussia (called the Franco-Prussian war), Paris was besieged twice, first by the Prussian army and later by French radicals who wanted to overthrow the new French government. Life was desperate for the Parisians. They nearly froze in the winter and had little to eat. They were terrorized by bombs and snipers.

Henry Dunant went into action. He collected clothing and blankets and gave them to needy people. He persuaded Prussian officials to release wounded prisoners.

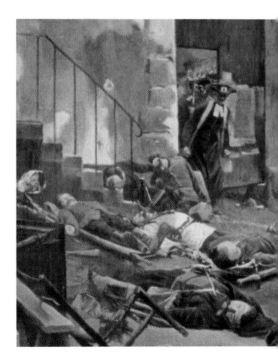

During the Franco-Prussian war, newly formed Red Cross societies stepped in to help.

When angry mobs ruled the city, he tried to reason with their leaders. Once he threw himself between a priest and an angry mob of radicals who saw the priest as a symbol of the authority they hated. Miraculously, Dunant saved himself and the priest.

By this time, many nations in Europe had already formed national Red Cross societies. As the Franco-Prussian war raged, the new societies proved their effectiveness. British and Dutch Red Cross workers were allowed to move freely across enemy lines. They quickly treated wounded Prussian soldiers and rushed them to hospitals.

By 1874, national societies had been established in 22 European countries. Soon the Red Cross movement spread to other continents. In 1876, the first red crescent appeared, in Turkey. In 1882, the United States signed the Geneva Convention—the last major nation to do so.

Over the following years, the Red Cross faced many more conflicts, and its work continued to expand. But people seemed to forget about Henry Dunant. He left Paris and for years lived in poverty in various cities in Europe. He became ill and spent three years in a hospital before he recovered.

In 1895, Dunant's life took yet another turn. A journalist visited him and wrote the story of his life. Suddenly, Dunant was respected again. Letters and money poured in. In 1901, he received the highest honor for humanitarian work—the Nobel Peace Prize. He lived to see another Geneva Convention adopted in 1906. He died in 1910.

As a result of Dunant's efforts, the world made significant advancements in human rights during his lifetime. His ideas were the foundation of the Red Cross movement, his enthusiasm its initial driving force. His dream, begun by a nightmarish battle, continues to save millions of lives.

Chapter Two

The Laws of Humanity

The Red Cross and Red Crescent movement is based on the belief that all human beings should be treated with respect, compassion, and consideration, even in times of conflict. The Red Cross and Red Crescent recognize seven fundamental principles: humanity, impartiality, neutrality, independence, voluntary service, unity, and universality. (These principles are explained on page 26.)

After the First Geneva Convention was adopted, the people of the Red Cross/Red Crescent developed three more conventions. They also developed two protocols (additions to the conventions). Between 1864 and 1949, the conventions were repeatedly restated and strengthened at international conferences. The fundamental principles of the Red Cross and Red Crescent movement are expressed many times in the conventions and protocols.

The Geneva Conventions

The four Geneva Conventions contain more than 400 articles governing the conduct of nations involved in armed conflicts. The conventions have been adopted—or ratified—by 186 nations; more than 100 countries have signed one or both of the protocols. No other international treaties have been so widely accepted.

Nations that ratify the conventions and protocols promise to abide by them. Each country is responsible for violations committed by its military officers and other individuals. Violators of the conventions and protocols may be subject to international sanctions, or punishments, such as the withdrawal of trade and loans.

The First Geneva Convention protects workers in war zones.

The First Geneva Convention, adopted in 1864, concerns care for the wounded and sick on the battlefield. It requires military forces to search for and collect the wounded, regardless of nationality, and to provide medical care for captured enemy soldiers. The convention protects medical and religious personnel so they may safely care for the wounded.

The Second Geneva Convention protects victims of war at sea.

Hospitals, ambulances, and medical equipment and supplies are also protected. The principles of humanity, impartiality, and neutrality are at work in this convention.

The Second Geneva Convention, first adopted in 1906, extends the protections of the First Convention to the seas. People who become sick or are wounded at sea, and people who are shipwrecked during a conflict, are protected under this convention.

The Third Geneva Convention was first adopted in 1929. It concerns the treatment of prisoners of war. It says POWs have the right to adequate food, clothing, shelter, and medical care. They have the right to send and receive family messages and to speak in private with ICRC delegates.

The Third Convention also says that detaining forces (people holding prisoners of war) must keep lists of their prisoners. They must recognize the right of prisoners to a trial. They must follow guidelines about the discipline of

Red Cross / Red Crescent Principles

Humanity
The international Red Cross and Red Crescent movement seeks to protect human life and health throughout the world. It seeks to prevent or at least lessen human suffering. And it works for peace.

Impartiality
The movement does not discriminate. It helps people based on their needs.

Neutrality
The movement does not take sides. Everyone—including people on different sides of a conflict—must be able to turn to Red Cross or Red Crescent workers with total trust.

prisoners. And they must obey rules about returning prisoners to the prisoners' own countries.

The Fourth Geneva Convention was adopted in 1949. It protects civilians. Civilians may not be detained or forced to leave a conflict area unless they are in danger. Certain actions—such as taking civilian hostages and recklessly destroying civilian lives and property—are not allowed.

The Fourth Convention also states that Red Cross/Red

Independence
The movement resists the influence of governments, political parties, and special interest groups.

Voluntary Service
Workers in the movement offer their help of their own free will.

Unity
There can be only one Red Cross/Red Crescent society in any one country. It must be open to all. It must help people throughout its territory.

Universality
The movement respects nations, but it works in any area, regardless of national boundaries.

Crescent societies must be allowed to do their work. This provision is based on the independence of the ICRC and the national societies.

The Protocols

In the years after 1949, many people saw a need to add new humanitarian laws to keep up with changes in the world. For example, the laws would deal with the use of new types of weapons—such as land mines and the atom bomb.

The ICRC developed two additions to the conventions. Called Protocols I and II, they were adopted in 1977. Although many nations have ratified the two additions, not all nations have done so. Nations that do not ratify agreements do not consider themselves bound by the agreements.

Protocol I concerns international armed conflicts. It prohibits random attacks against civilians and the things civilians need to survive, such as crops and livestock. The Protocol prohibits massive air bombardments, such as those that caused millions of deaths in World War II. The parties involved in the conflict must provide medical aid and food to civilians. If they cannot, they must allow the ICRC to do so. Protocol II extends the provisions of Protocol I to noninternational armed conflicts such as civil wars.

An old adage says "All's fair in love and war." The Geneva Conventions and Protocols I and II embody a different idea—that all is not fair in war. In protecting victims of armed conflict, they represent real progress since the days of Solferino.

Chapter Three

A World in Need

Albert Schweitzer, a great humanitarian and winner of the Nobel Peace Prize, once called the Red Cross "a light showing the right way in darkness." The Red Cross/Red Crescent reaches out to those who struggle to survive, those with few means to make their lives better. Such people are defined by the Red Cross/Red Crescent as "vulnerable." The ICRC and the Federation now consider two billion people to be vulnerable.

How do so many people become vulnerable? Usually they are the victims of a widespread and long-term disaster, such as war or famine. Many such people become refugees, fleeing their homelands. In the 1990s, the flight of large numbers of people has become a serious global problem. Yet another global problem is the spread of AIDS.

The Cruelty of Conflict

During the 1990s, about 40 wars were fought around the globe. In the Middle East, war affected Iraq, Israel, Jordan, Kuwait, Syria, and others. In Europe, civil wars tore apart the nations formed from the former Yugoslavia (Slovenia, Croatia, Macedonia, and Bosnia-Herzegovina, which is sometimes called Bosnia). Afghanistan, Sri Lanka, Tajikistan, Cambodia, and other Asian nations have endured conflicts. In Latin America, civil wars in El Salvador, Guatemala, Nicaragua, and Peru have been terribly damaging.

A sad result of warfare is civilian casualties—injuries and deaths of nonsoldiers. Land mines cause many of these casualties. Too often, civilians such as women gathering firewood and children playing are the victims of these cruel weapons.

"The Human Disaster"

Famine is the most serious ongoing problem facing the Red Cross/Red Crescent. The Red Cross/Red Crescent predicts that 6.5 billion people—85 percent of the world's population—will know hunger by the year 2000.

Famine sometimes has natural causes. For example, floods or drought (a long period without rain) can make farming nearly impossible. But famine is sometimes called the "human disaster" because it is often human-made—caused by armed conflict, population growth, and the misuse of land. In many places, such as Sudan in Africa, populations are growing. When too many people live in an area, fertile land becomes scarce. Some farmers may allow too many animals to graze on the little land available.

Worst of all, people cut down trees in forests for firewood, dwellings, and other uses. When large areas are stripped of trees (a process called deforestation), drought often follows. Trees help hold the moisture from rainfall; without trees and other vegetation, moisture evaporates quickly. In addition, the deep roots of trees help to keep topsoil from eroding—blowing or washing away. When too many trees are cut down, land soon becomes barren and useless. Crops won't grow, and people begin to starve.

Like other countries in Africa, Sudan has experienced repeated cycles of drought and famine during the past few decades. Each year millions of Sudanese people face starvation. Regina Frisch, a Red Cross volunteer in Sudan, saw the effects of famine firsthand. In her diary, she wrote:

15 *November*
Winter has come. At night, the temperature is below zero [32° Fahrenheit]. Many of the children we have been attending to in Sindi, the village where we are spending the night, do not even have a shirt to cover their emaciated bodies. Hassan, a two-year-old, struggled to breathe and had a high temperature. His mother could not hold him; she was too weak. I wrapped him in a blanket and placed him in the arms of his grandfather. Nevertheless, Hassan died at two o'clock in the morning.

Thousands of people from Bosnia-Herzegovina have fled war between Serbian forces on one side and Croat and Muslim forces on the other.

Refugees

When war is raging around them, people are often forced to flee. Their own homes or those of their neighbors may have been destroyed; family members or friends may have been killed by bombs or bullets from nearby fighting. They have no choice but to leave home to seek safety elsewhere.

Like warfare, famine also forces many people to flee their homes. People who flee their nations are called *refugees*. Some people are forced out of their homes but remain within their own nations. The Red Cross/Red Crescent refers to them as *internally displaced people*.

Refugees and internally displaced people don't know whether they will be away from home for a day, a year—or forever. In most cases, they have nowhere to go and few means to obtain food or other necessities.

The flight of refugees and internally displaced people is a significant problem. In 1995, as many as 42 million people were refugees or displaced people. More than half of all refugees and displaced people are children.

AIDS: Nowhere to Hide

One of the most difficult problems faced by Red Cross and Red Crescent societies is the growing AIDS epidemic. The number of people who have AIDS and who carry the human immunodeficiency virus is increasing at an alarming rate. AIDS is often—but not always—related to drug use and sexual behavior. These factors exist in the largest cities and the smallest villages everywhere.

No one agrees on the exact numbers of people with AIDS and HIV. The World Health Organization estimated in the early 1990s that about 350,000 people had AIDS and as many as 10 million were infected by HIV. By the year 2000, 6 million people may have AIDS, and 25 to 30 million people may be HIV positive (infected by HIV).

AIDS is particularly devastating in poor countries (sometimes called *developing countries*). "Poor countries seem to be particularly ill-equipped to check this deadly phenomenon," said Dr. Anne Petitgirard, AIDS program director for the Federation. Several factors make people in such countries more vulnerable to AIDS. First, HIV is carried in a person's blood, so it can be transmitted by blood transfusions (when blood from one person is given to another). In poor countries, noncontaminated blood supplies may be scarce. Second, medical care may be poor. Finally, education may be poor. People may not understand that HIV can be transmitted by sexual behaviors or by sharing needles (as sometimes happens when people take illegal drugs).

Although developing countries are hardest hit by the AIDS epidemic, no country is immune to it. In the United States, more than one million people are HIV positive. One-fourth to one-half of them will develop AIDS during the next seven years. Already nearly 200,000 Americans have died from AIDS.

AIDS threatens all people. According to Anne Petitgirard, "AIDS is an emergency—an emergency which is going to last a long time."

The Agony of Africa

Nowhere do these global problems—conflict, famine, the flight of masses of people, and AIDS—come together more devastatingly than in Africa. And nowhere is the work of the Red Cross/Red Crescent more needed. Throughout the 1980s and into the 1990s, the problems on this continent have been chief concerns for the Red Cross/Red Crescent. In fact, more than half the work done by the ICRC and the Federation each year addresses the critical needs of Africa's people.

The AIDS epidemic has already become a disaster in Africa: About 10 million Africans (1 out of 70) are infected by HIV. Famine, too, stalks many Africans; more than 25 million people in Africa went hungry in 1994.

In addition, years of civil wars and other kinds of strife have kept Angola, Ethiopia, Liberia, Mozambique, Rwanda, Somalia, Sudan, and other African countries in turmoil. Thousands of people have been killed and wounded in these conflicts. Millions of Africans have become refugees. In fact, one third of the world's refugees and more than half of its displaced people are in Africa.

One troubled African nation is Somalia. This country on the eastern coast of the continent has endured years of fighting among clans. No one government is in power. More than 500,000 of Somalia's six million people have died since 1991 (when the national government collapsed) from violence, hunger, and disease. One-third of the population is homeless, and millions of Somalis are vulnerable—poor and starving.

Rwanda, another African nation, has suffered from fighting by two tribal groups—the Hutus (who are in the majority) and the Tutsis—since 1990. Dr. John Sundin, an American Red Cross surgeon, worked in Kigali, Rwanda, for two months in 1994 during a brutal outbreak of fighting. In his diary, Sundin wrote:

> I'm living and working at a Red Cross field hospital that was set up a month ago . . . . We have about two hundred patients staying on the floor and in tents. I am the surgeon, and work with two nurses in our two

Africa

Many African nations have struggled to solve the problems of war, famine, and the AIDS epidemic.

operating rooms, which were classrooms a month ago . . . . I've done maybe twenty amputations of legs, hands, and an eye over the last week.

May 25
Bunkered in today. Mortar hit Red Cross compound next door, killing two and wounding five. Hospital staff leaves and wounded pour in. Fifty more today. Putting them everywhere on the ground now. No more tents . . . . Twenty cases to operate on but tomorrow will be another day of shelling.

June 11
Yesterday we had fifteen cases between 9 A.M. and 1 P.M. Arms and legs to cut off or dress, a nose and two eyes blown away, a five-year-old leg connected by a thread of flesh . . . . I used to know the patients. Now there are so many wounded that it's assembly-line first aid.

Relief efforts in Africa have been hampered in several ways. A lack of worldwide interest in the Africans' desperate situation has made fund-raising difficult. The world's attention has often been focused on other crises, such as the Persian Gulf War of 1991 and the turmoil in Bosnia in eastern Europe.

Relief efforts have met additional obstacles in some nations. In Somalia, fighting has kept relief workers from reaching troubled areas. Some ICRC delegates have been killed or wounded delivering relief supplies.

Finally, relief agencies have had problems working together. For example, in Somalia, the ICRC and another agency disagreed over the best way to deliver food to starving Somalis. In Angola, a group that opposed the government refused to cooperate with the national Red Cross society.

How do Red Cross/Red Crescent workers face the enormous tasks in Africa and elsewhere? John Sundin often felt at a loss during his time in Rwanda. He wrote, "The terrible reality of this [hospital] camp overwhelms me." Even so, he managed to keep hope. He explained, "I hear the Rwandans gathered for church services, their hymns drifting through the compound. Who am I not to have hope when they have so much of it themselves?"

Africa seems to be plagued with disasters. The situation seems overwhelming, but the ICRC doesn't give up. "We shall not abandon Africa!" declared ICRC president Cornelio Sommaruga.

Throughout the world, thousands of people live in darkness—the darkness of fear, homelessness, insecurity, hunger, and disease. In the next few chapters, you will read about how Red Cross and Red Crescent workers bring light to the lives of many of these people.

Chapter Four

The ICRC *in* Action

The story of Angola, a country in southwestern Africa, gives an idea of the magnitude of ICRC operations. Pierre Gauthier, an ICRC delegate, worked in Angola in 1990 and 1991. At that time, the country had been engaged for 16 years in a bloody civil war between government forces and a powerful opposition movement called UNITA. The ICRC had been working in the country since 1979.

Gauthier's first mission was a "cross-line operation"—crossing the front lines of battle. Though dangerous, the mission was necessary. Due to damaged roads, the constant fighting, and land mines, people in remote areas could not travel. They were stranded and starving.

In October 1990, Gauthier and two other ICRC workers accompanied a convoy of nine trucks of supplies enroute to the remote village of Gove, Angola. Gauthier and his companions knew that many land mines were buried along the route. As their trucks bumped over the pitted roads, the group worried constantly about the mines.

Fortunately, the convoy made it safely to Gove. There, the delegates distributed food, blankets, soap, and other supplies to 2,000 families in the village. Gauthier especially remembered one child in the line of people waiting to receive supplies. He wrote: "How old is that little girl? Ten years, twelve at most. She waits calmly in line for her

A convoy of supply trucks made a dangerous trip in Angola in 1991.

turn. . . . Now she is in front of me. Now it is her turn to receive her portion of corn and bean seeds. . . . As I give her the signal to approach, she looks at me and hesitates a moment; then a wonderful smile lights up her face."

During the war, the ICRC evacuated thousands of wounded and seriously ill people to area hospitals. ICRC delegates trained staff to operate first aid posts in the Angolan cities of Huambo, Bié, and Benguela. Many people lost limbs in the war; ICRC orthopedic centers produced 11,000 prostheses, or artificial limbs, for them.

Pierre Gauthier and other ICRC workers brought food to remote villages in Angola.

Emergency relief for people in war-torn nations is a chief task of the ICRC.

ICRC workers also forwarded thousands of messages to families split up by the fighting. They repaired hundreds of wells. Between 1979 and 1991, the ICRC negotiated the release of 3,000 prisoners of war.

Because travel overland was so difficult, most relief supplies were flown in—shipped on large transport planes to Angola itself, then on smaller craft to the country's towns and villages.

In 1991, a peace accord sponsored by the United Nations halted the fighting in Angola. With peace came the beginnings of a new way of life. The ICRC remained in Angola. It gradually decreased its emergency relief operations and began to distribute farm tools and seeds.

It also helped the large numbers of people looking for missing family members. It continued to negotiate for the release of prisoners of war (about a thousand were still being held) and to supply artificial limbs for wounded people. ICRC workers also began to conduct courses in international humanitarian law to help ensure a lasting peace.

Even so, in 1993, the civil war resumed. For a country just beginning to recover from so many years of constant warfare, this new outbreak of violence was devastating. Immediately the ICRC began to supply emergency relief again—striving to meet the needs of this new crisis.

The Lifeline of Relief

Pierre Gauthier and other ICRC workers made a dangerous journey to take supplies to the people of Gove in Angola. Typically, more than half of the ICRC's work during a year involves emergency relief—supplying food, shelter, clothing, water, and medical supplies. Sometimes this emergency relief work lasts for years.

Somalia has been one of the ICRC's most demanding projects in terms of relief. The lack of any government in this African nation has allowed gangs to thrive. These gangs, based on clan loyalties, rove the countryside looting and shooting. The gangs have attacked trucks carrying sacks of rice and other food and supplies. Sometimes when relief organizations distribute food, gangs move in to take it, fighting each other or attacking the guards protecting the supplies.

Because of the danger posed by these gangs, the people of the Red Cross/Red Crescent have often been alone in providing relief in Somalia. They overcame some of the difficulty by making agreements with clan leaders. They also set up communal kitchens, where food was cooked on the spot. The gangs were far less likely to take a pot of hot soup or cooked rice than to take sacks of rice.

Another huge task in a place like Somalia is supplying clean water. Clean water is the "absolute number one priority," according to an ICRC report. Often clean water must come before any other kind of relief, since people need drinking water even before they need food. The water must be pure; contaminated water can spread disease and even cause deaths.

Hospitals especially need tremendous amounts of water—more than 150 quarts per patient per day, plus 100 quarts for each surgical operation. The water is used for drinking and washing, and for sterilizing equipment.

Among the ICRC's first tasks in Somalia in 1991 was the repair of the water supply system in a hospital in the town of Berbera. ICRC teams also distributed water to villagers and dug wells on the outskirts of town.

In 1991, war in Iraq damaged that nation's water supplies. For several weeks, Iraqis were without clean water. ICRC delegates distributed more than seven million bags of "Red Cross water" (as the Iraqis called it). The first stops for the water bags were hospitals and health centers. Meanwhile, the ICRC worked with engineers and other workers from many different national Red Cross and Red Crescent societies to build temporary water tanks and to repair Iraq's permanent water supply system.

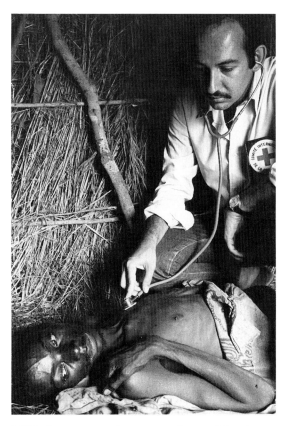

ICRC doctors care for many who would not receive medical help otherwise.

Caring for the Sick and Wounded

Almost half of the ICRC's field workers are engaged in medical services. The ICRC steps in when local health services have broken down or become overburdened, with too many sick or wounded to care for. The ICRC sends doctors, nurses, other medical workers, medical equipment, and medicine to conflict zones. One of the main tasks of ICRC medical teams is war surgery. In 1993, doctors at ICRC hospitals performed 22,572 operations in eight countries. ICRC medical teams face grueling conditions in many countries: hazardous travel, freezing or baking temperatures, an unending flow of wounded people, and the terror of being fired upon.

During the 1980s, Peru suffered years of civil war between its government and antigovernment forces. Many Peruvians, already poor and living in remote mountainous areas or jungles, were trapped by the fighting and by destroyed roads. People who became ill or were injured by the violence could not reach hospitals.

Beginning in 1985, the ICRC set up more than 200 health posts, or clinics, throughout the country. Some of the posts could be reached only by donkey or on foot. Traveling over rocky mountain paths and through jungles, ICRC teams carried first aid supplies and medicines to the posts. For many Peruvians, the ICRC posts have been the only source of medical care for many years.

Another important medical program of the ICRC helps war victims who have lost limbs. Most of these victims have been injured by land mines. The program began in 1970; it now includes 29 orthopedic centers in 17 countries. The centers are located in or near areas of current or recent conflict, such as Sudan, Cambodia, Iraq, and other countries.

Technicians in the centers make wheelchairs and crutches. They also make many kinds of prostheses to replace missing legs or arms and orthoses, devices to support paralyzed limbs. The centers also teach local people to make these devices. In most cases, the devices are designed to be easy to repair or replace.

Protecting Prisoners of War

When enemy soldiers are captured during a conflict, they are often held as prisoners as war. The ICRC protects POWs in several ways. Countries that have signed the Third Geneva Convention have obligations to their prisoners of war. The convention doesn't include rules about why a person can be detained. But it does say POWs have the right to be held safely and humanely. The convention specifies that prisoners have the right to be visited by ICRC delegates. POWs may also receive and send messages through the ICRC.

In 1994, ICRC delegates visited more than 99,000 prisoners in 55 countries. When ICRC delegates visit prisoners, they interview them and investigate the conditions of their imprisonment. When allowed, ICRC doctors also visit prisoners.

The Third Geneva Convention gives the ICRC the responsibility of reporting prisoners' concerns to prison authorities. The delegates follow up each case to make sure a prisoner's rights are upheld.

The ICRC can point out violations of prisoners' rights, but it has no power to force governments to honor those rights. For example, when delegates learn of torture and other ill treatment, they strongly urge prison authorities to stop such practices. But they have no power to remove the prisoners or to stop the torture.

ICRC delegates report their findings to the government holding the prisoners. Sometimes they also report to the prisoners' home countries. The ICRC reports do not condemn governments, and they are not made public. The purpose of the reports is to explain prisoners' conditions, not to question the reasons for their imprisonment.

Reuniting People

"Dearest Son," the letter read, "We are all fine but worry about you as there has been no news for what seems like a lifetime. After nearly two years of searching and

Heavy shelling of Sarajevo in Bosnia-Herzegovina reduced this neighborhood to rubble.

asking everyone, the Red Cross people finally told us you are still alive."

Few people could imagine the effect this message had on Samir, the missing son. He had been captured while fighting in the brutal, three-way conflict in his country, Bosnia. Samir was one of thousands of POWs held by either Croatian, Serbian, or Bosnian government forces.

While Samir's family in Sarajevo, Bosnia's capital, had worried about his fate, he had wondered about theirs. He hadn't known whether they had survived the shelling of the city by the Serbs in 1992. Thanks to the ICRC's Central Tracing Agency (CTA), he finally received the letter from his family. The heaviness in his heart was lightened that day.

During times of war, communications break down. Families can be separated and have no way to contact one another. Soldiers can disappear in the chaos of battle. Their families may not know if they have been captured or killed—or if they are alive and well. The Central Tracing Agency (CTA)

ICRC delegates visited prisoners of war in Russia.

of the ICRC provides the vital service of delivering messages and finding missing people.

In Somalia, telephone and postal services collapsed during its civil war. Many ordinary people were forced to flee their homes. Their relatives were desperate for news of them. In 1992 alone, the CTA and the Somali Red Crescent handled 223,000 family messages for Somalis.

Spreading the Word

An important mission of the ICRC is to explain the Geneva Conventions, the fundamental principles of the Red Cross/Red Crescent, and the importance of the Red Cross and Red Crescent emblems. Often the ICRC trains local Red Cross or Red Crescent societies to spread this information.

Explaining principles such as neutrality is not always easy. In war-torn countries, people are often suspicious and hostile. They wonder, "Why does the Red Cross or Red Crescent help our enemies?"

Dr. Joël Lagroutte, an ICRC delegate, faced this problem when he spoke to a group of villagers in the African country of Uganda. How could he explain neutrality to them?

"What would you do if you found me on the edge of your village, having been knocked down by a car?" he asked them. The villagers answered that they would help him, even though they didn't know who he was, what he wanted, or why he was in their village.

"That's just what my organization, the Red Cross, is all about," he said, "helping someone like me, someone who's not fighting—or in any case not fighting any longer—and who needs someone else's help."

Chapter Five

The International Federation

Volcanic eruption in the Philippines! Earthquake in Afghanistan! Floods in Cambodia! Once a week, a sudden natural disaster strikes somewhere in the world. Some disasters are so terrible that the Red Cross or Red Crescent society in the country where the disaster happens calls for international help. The International Federation of Red Cross and Red Crescent Societies steps in, bringing Red Cross/Red Crescent volunteers from many countries together to speed relief to a stricken area.

Working through the national societies, the Federation takes medical supplies and food to the victims of disasters and sets up emergency housing for them. In 1994, nearly 19 million people in 46 countries received emergency relief through the Federation. The cost: $333 million. The year before, 1993, the Federation helped 15 million people at a cost of $363 million.

Another task of the Federation is preparing for disasters. Hurricanes and earthquakes can't be prevented. But injury, death, and the destruction of property from such disasters often can be.

The cyclones of Bangladesh illustrate the importance of disaster preparedness. Seven million people live

Survivors of a 1991 cyclone in Bangladesh reached up to catch boxes of crackers from a relief helicopter.

along the stormy southern coast of the country where cyclones most frequently occur. After one cyclone in 1970 killed half a million people, the Federation and the Bangladesh Red Crescent Society began a Cyclone Preparedness Programme (CPP). The CPP built 62 concrete shelters (or "armored beasts," as residents called them).

Most of the Bangladeshis in the coastal region live in small, remote villages. Most do not own radios or televisions. Warning them of a coming storm is often difficult. To give these people time to reach the shelters, the CPP developed a special early warning system. The system broadcasts news of a storm on the radio, but it also signals the danger with sirens and flags. Nearly 27,000 volunteers also spread warnings by word of mouth among those who might not receive word otherwise.

A cyclone shelter

Even with the early warning system in place, when another severe cyclone and tidal waves hit Bangladesh in April 1991, an estimated 140,000 died. Yet thousands more might have died without the CPP.

The CPP continued to build shelters in the following years. When another severe storm hit in May 1994, about 750,000 people found safety in 225 shelters. Only an estimated 100 to 200 people died. The 1994 cyclone did not cause tidal waves, so luck certainly played a part. But without a doubt, the CPP also played a big role in bringing about this vast improvement over the earlier disasters.

Once the immediate effects of a disaster have passed, the Federation provides ongoing help in a devastated area. It helps communities restore their telephones lines, roads, and water supplies.

Preventing Hunger

Regina Frisch, the Red Cross nurse who served in Sudan, had to watch two-year-old Hassan die of starvation. The Federation does everything it can to prevent such tragedies. When people face slowly developing disasters such as famine, the Federation not only provides emergency relief but also seeks long-term solutions.

In Ethiopia, the Federation has been working with the Ethiopian Red Cross Society (ERCS) to fight famine. This African nation struggles because of poor economic development, a growing population, and increasing numbers of vulnerable people (including refugees, internally displaced people, and the rural poor). In the struggle to end famine, Ethiopians face overwhelming odds.

The ERCS and the Federation began to teach farmers new planting methods, including ways to rotate crops (changing crops and planting different fields from year to year to keep soil fertile). The organizations also replanted trees in areas where they had been cut down. In a dry land like Ethiopia, trees are especially important in retaining moisture and soil. Replanting forests is a crucial step in preventing drought—and thus famine.

In spite of these efforts, Ethiopians continue to starve. Every year the country produces less food. The people of

Ethiopia depend more and more on the Federation and other organizations for help. Their situation illustrates the enormous challenge in solving the complex problem of famine.

Aid for Refugees

The ICRC aids refugees and displaced people within areas of conflict; the Federation helps those who have fled a conflict or a disaster. The Federation works closely with the Office of the United Nations High Commissioner for Refugees (UNHCR) to help millions of refugees every year.

Since 1990, ongoing conflict in the African country of Rwanda has led many of its people to flee to surrounding countries. In 1994, two million Rwandans fled to Burundi, Uganda, Zaire, and Tanzania. A single massive wave of 200,000 Rwandan people crossed the border into Tanzania near the town of Ngara. Within hours, the Federation and the Tanzanian Red Cross were on the scene.

"We had trained action teams and volunteers ready," said Sheila Wilson, head of the Federation's delegation in Tanzania. "We knew what to do, and we knew we could do it." The teams quickly set up a camp near Ngara where the refugees could live. With 200,000 people to shelter, Benaco (as the camp was called) became the largest refugee camp in the world.

Rwanda

Tanzania

Sheila Wilson

A German Red Cross team set up a camp hospital. Another German team provided drinking water. Within two weeks of its creation, Benaco was running smoothly.

Another operation, this one in Sudan, took place in 1989–1990. Many people had been displaced by civil war in that African nation. Since most of the fighting was just to the south of a tiny village called Abyei, the village was a natural refuge. People had poured into Abyei until its numbers had swollen to more than 40,000. Abyei had become a refugee camp. Its new residents had no means of obtaining food.

Together with the Sudanese Red Crescent, the Federation stepped in. One Federation worker from the United States, Robert Joy, was given the job of helping the Sudanese Red Crescent determine the best way to distribute sorghum (a grain), beans, and other food to the people of Abyei.

In a diary, Joy described his arrival in the village. "The first wonderful thing is the children," he wrote. "They cluster around us, reaching, touching, smiling." So many

Thousands of Rwandans fled to Tanzania in 1994.

people reached for his hand, said Joy, that "it is possible to shake and squeeze hands continuously."

To distribute the food, Joy divided a field into two areas—one for piles of sorghum and beans and one for the people waiting to receive the food. Each family received a registration card marked with the amount of food to be given them. Joy wrote:

> The chiefs of the people bring them to the field early in the morning and form them into groups. Most of them are women, some with children. They will sit patiently in the open sun for up to eight hours awaiting their turn. . . . The people are allowed to approach . . . several at a time, where they present the registration card each family has been given. These cards each tell a story of creases, dirt, oil stains, fingermarks.

Joy watched as families brought sacks, hollow gourds, and baskets to the waiting piles of food. According to Joy, the procedure was "laborious, repetitive;" in all, it took five days. Temperatures rose above 120 degrees Fahrenheit. Even so, wrote Joy, relief workers sang as they filled the many containers with the lifesaving food.

Focus on AIDS

Since 1987, the Federation has considered AIDS to be a worldwide disaster. The Federation focuses on education—about the disease and its prevention, and about the people who have it. The Federation promotes human

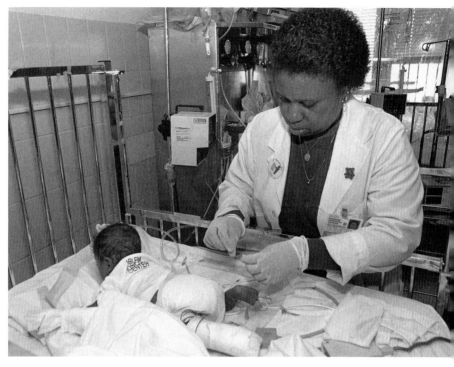

A nurse in New York City tended a baby with AIDS. The Federation educates people about the prevention of this deadly disease.

rights for people with AIDS and fights discrimination against people infected by HIV.

The Federation acts in both large and small ways to prevent the spread of AIDS. At the global level, it works with the World Health Organization and other agencies to educate the public. At the same time, Red Cross and Red Crescent volunteers are working within their own communities to change attitudes and behavior, one person at a time.

In 1990, the Federation, in partnership with the World Organization of the Scout Movement, produced an AIDS training manual for Red Cross/Red Crescent youth workers. The manual offers practical suggestions to help the youth workers lead the way in the fight against AIDS. It explains how to involve a Red Cross/Red Crescent youth group in community health programs.

One interesting idea described in the manual is to write a play about AIDS using puppets as the main characters. Using puppets is useful since many issues related to AIDS "can be either embarrassing or difficult to discuss openly," the manual explains.

Another Federation AIDS project is a booklet called *Caring for People with AIDS at Home.* The booklet grew out of a program developed by the Norwegian Red Cross and several national societies in Africa. The booklet teaches families the basics of home care for people living with AIDS. It gives practical and humane advice on everything from hygiene in the home to preparing for death.

The Federation is in a unique position to prevent AIDS. As an alliance of national societies in more than 160 nations, it reaches people around the world. It works in both urban and rural areas. As one Federation official put it, "We are everywhere."

AIDs and other problems cannot be easily solved. But the Federation continues to follow the mission described by its founder, Henry P. Davison: to be "a permanent worldwide crusade to improve health, prevent sickness, and alleviate suffering."

Chapter Six

The National Societies

Late one night in 1988, members of a Kentucky church youth group were on their way home from a trip to Cincinnati, Ohio, when their bus was hit by a drunk driver. Tragically, 24 children and 3 adults died.

Within hours of the accident, disaster specialists from the Cincinnati Red Cross—including members of the Crisis Support Nursing Team (CSNT)—responded. Trena Goodwin, one of the CSNT nurses, said team members learned that many of the survivors had been taken to area hospitals. Families of the group waited anxiously for news about their loved ones. But no one knew who had been taken to hospitals and who had died. "Since none of the bodies had yet been identified," Goodwin said, "we could not tell the families . . . whether their children were among the dead."

A tragic crash in 1988 brought American Red
Cross nurses to counsel families of the victims.

History of the American Red Cross

The American Red Cross was founded in 1881 by Clara Barton. Barton cared for wounded soldiers during the Civil War (1861–1865) in the United States. Then she traveled to Europe to aid civilians during the Franco-Prussian war of 1870–1871 (the same war in which Henry Dunant saved lives).

In Europe, Barton learned about the international Red Cross movement. When she returned home, she tried unsuccessfully to persuade the U.S. government to join the movement. In 1881, she founded the American Association of the Red Cross. A year later, the U.S. Senate finally ratified the First Geneva Convention—the 32nd nation to do so.

By the time the families learned the fate of their children, they were exhausted, hungry, and in a state of shock. Since the CSNT focuses on dealing with the psychological reactions of disaster victims and their families, the nurses quickly put their skills to work, counseling and comforting them.

"As is the case with most disasters," said Goodwin, "we found it incredible to see so many lives altered forever."

The CSNT nurses are part of the American Red Cross (ARC), a national society of the Red Cross/Red Crescent. ARC's motto is "Help Can't Wait." The American Red Cross has more than one million members in 1,800 active chapters. In a recent year, ARC Disaster Services responded to 60,000 disasters—from house fires to floods to earthquakes.

Most countries have a national Red Cross or Red Crescent society. New societies are constantly forming as the political map changes. For example, the former Soviet Union, once a huge nation reaching across Asia to Europe, has broken up into many smaller, independent countries. These nations are now forming their own national Red Cross societies.

National societies tackle their countries' most pressing problems, which vary from country to country. Almost always, though, their most important work is to respond to sudden accidents or natural disasters.

The diverse projects of the national societies include health and safety programs, blood donation programs, community development, and social services. For example, each year about 4 million Americans donate blood through the American Red Cross, giving a total of about half the nation's blood supply. More than 11 million Americans take ARC courses in first aid, cardiopulmonary resuscitation (CPR), and water safety.

Some programs of national societies reach across oceans to help people in other countries. In Cambodia in Southeast Asia, several million land mines remain since the years of the Vietnam War. As many as 36,000 Cambodians have lost arms, legs, hands, or feet when mines have exploded near them.

Since 1991, the American Red Cross has run an orthopedic center in the country's Komong Speu province. It

About 60 people are killed each month by land mines in Cambodia. Many more people, like this child, are wounded.

Land Mines

They are "fighters that never miss, strike blindly, do not carry weapons openly, and go on killing long after hostilities are ended." That's how one ICRC delegate described a deadly modern weapon: land mines.

Land mines are devices that explode when they are stepped on or when a wire is pulled. They are hidden in the ground, under brush, and in trees.

An estimated 100 million land mines are buried or hidden in current and recent conflict zones around the world. An estimated 10 million may be in Afghanistan, 3 to 6 million in Croatia and Bosnia-Herzegovina, and as many as 4 million in Cambodia.

In 1993, the ICRC launched an international appeal to end the use of land mines. International laws forbid the use of land mines, but those laws are difficult to enforce. Many nations that manufacture and plant land mines do not recognize international weapons treaties.

As it pushes for stronger international laws, the ICRC is also informing the public about the cruelty of these weapons. Meanwhile, it assists the victims of land mines and helps remove mines wherever possible.

works closely with the Cambodian Red Cross, the Australian Red Cross, and the Swiss Red Cross. At the center, ARC medical workers train Cambodians in making prostheses for the victims of the mines. Soon the training will be complete, and the center in Komong Speu will be turned over to the Cambodians to run themselves.

National Societies around the World

The following projects are just a few of the many carried out by national societies of the Red Cross/Red Crescent.

In Southeast Asia, the **Thai Red Cross** and the World Health Organization are testing a new vaccine for HIV. Thailand has a special interest in curing AIDS. Just 64 cases were reported in Thailand in 1990; however, by 1994, the number was over 3,000.

In the Far East, the **Singapore Red Cross** has an active training program for youth. Every Saturday, scores of kids head for the Singapore Red Cross headquarters, where they teach and take courses in first aid, leadership, and other subjects. The Singapore Red Cross has identified common health problems among Singapore youth—including stress, smoking, drug abuse, and lack of exercise—and educates young people about them.

The **Ethiopian Red Cross Society** sent three youth workers around the country in 1990 to train Ethiopians in first aid. Two of the young people were from Finland; the third was from Ethiopia.

One of the youth workers said the enormous task was "hard and slow. It takes 26 days to properly train a first

aid worker, and then we start all over again." But the re-
sults were worth it: Hundreds of Ethiopians learned the
basics of first aid.

In North America, the **Canadian Red Cross Society**
conducts a "Summer Safety" program on ferry boats traveling the nation's eastern shore. The program uses the-
ater, mime, and songs to teach cold water survival and
water rescue techniques. Instructors also explain first aid
for choking and for heart attacks and talk about Red
Cross principles.

In Latin America, the **Honduran Red Cross** (HRC) is playing a unique role in its country's blood program. Until the
early 1990s, commercial blood banks there paid people
to give blood. But paying people to donate blood can be
dangerous. Blood donors, eager to earn money, may not
reveal that they carry HIV or other blood-related diseases.
Their blood would be extremely dangerous—deadly in

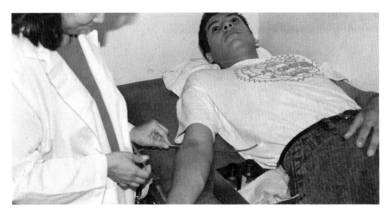

The Honduran Red Cross began a voluntary blood donation
program.

the case of HIV—to people receiving it by transfusion. To overcome this danger, the HRC established a single national blood management system based on voluntary donation.

In another Latin American country, the **Mexican Red Cross** (MRC) responded to a huge gas explosion in the city of Guadalajara in 1993. A team of trained rescue workers acted quickly and smoothly, in contrast to a chaotic response to Hurricane Gilbert, which struck Mexico in 1988. The difference? The MRC had adopted the American Red Cross's Disaster Response System, called the "3000 Series." The series consists of instructional materials covering more than 100 aspects of disaster response. Red Cross societies in other Latin American countries—including Colombia, Costa Rica, Ecuador, El Salvador, Jamaica, and Venezuela—also use the series.

Chapter Seven

Keep the Light Burning

very year the world's needs are greater. And every
year the appeals to the Red Cross/Red Crescent for
help don't simply increase—they double. How will
the Red Cross/Red Crescent movement respond?

The Federation will continue to sponsor projects
aimed at preventing and preparing for disasters. Planting
trees in Ethiopia, for example, may help avert drought.
Early warning systems—such as the one in Bangladesh—
may save lives during storms. The ICRC will continue to
educate people about humanitarian principles.

The greatest hope for the future, however, may lie with
the youth of the world. If the international Red Cross/Red
Crescent movement is a "light showing the right way in

darkness," the young people of the movement are the keepers of that light.

Red Cross Youth around the World

About 90 million young people ages 5 to 25 are part of the Red Cross/Red Crescent movement. Many of them are involved in Red Cross or Red Crescent programs in their schools. Others belong to Red Cross and Red Crescent Youth (RCY) programs at the national or international level.

Red Cross/Red Crescent youth do many different things. Sometimes they risk their lives in dangerous conflict zones; sometimes they leap in to help after a natural disaster. Following are some examples of recent RCY projects:

- In Lebanon, Red Cross Youth transported and treated wounded victims of conflict.
- In Malaysia, Red Cross Youth prepared daily meals for three months for 800 people whose village had been destroyed by a factory explosion.
- In Poland, Red Cross Youth organized summer camps for 600 children from Chernobyl, Ukraine (the site of a nuclear accident in 1986).
- In El Salvador, Red Cross Youth packed "Family Bags" of supplies for earthquake victims.
- In the Republic of Korea, Red Cross Youth hosted an International Peace Camp with young people from 15 countries.

Young Red Cross volunteers are also active in the United States. Michelle Walley, the Red Cross volunteer who joined the rescue effort after the bombing in Oklahoma City, became a member of the Disaster Action Team (DAT) of the local Red Cross when she was 15. DAT members are specially trained to respond to emergencies such as fires, floods, earthquakes—and bombings.

In Seattle, Washington, a youth group raised nearly $36,000 in eight weeks. Most of the money went to help the victims of an earthquake in Kobe, Japan. In Chicago, Illinois, young Red Cross volunteers taught AIDS awareness to more than 10,000 local teenagers. In Louisville, Kentucky, kids ages 8 to 12 provide services to elderly people. Their older brothers and sisters—ages 13 to 18—become trained volunteers in community agencies.

The American Red Cross sponsors two international programs especially for young people. One is the Friendship Box Program. Groups of young people fill small boxes with pens, small dolls, toothbrushes, soap, hair clips, and other items and send them to needy children in the United States and abroad. Some children make finger puppets, bookmarks, and greeting cards to enclose. Each friendship box is a gift from one child to another.

A similar project is the School Chest Program. Students construct a wooden chest (about four cubic feet in size). Then they fill it with school supplies (notepads, rules, pencils and sharpeners, and other things)—enough for a class of 24 students. Sometimes the chests also include

Somali students display gifts of friendship from students in the United States.

toothbrushes, first aid kits, soccer balls, and games. Like the friendship boxes, the school chests can then be sent next door—or across the world.

Keepers of the Future

Young people have been involved in the Red Cross and Red Crescent movement since 1914, when national societies began to establish youth sections. In the 1990s, nearly every Red Cross and Red Crescent chapter has a youth section.

The youth section is an important part of each national society. In some societies, in fact, young people make up most of the membership. The international Red Cross/Red Crescent youth program has four main goals. First, the program educates youth about health-related subjects. Second, it promotes community service. Third, it fosters international understanding. Finally, it asks young people to tell others about the fundamental principles of the Red Cross/Red Crescent.

Sala Ilaria of Treviso, Italy, was an RCY member when she was in her teens and early 20s. Through the RCY program, she met many people who shared her belief in "help for our neighbors for a better world."

One role of young people in the Red Cross/Red Crescent, she said, is "to organize a chain of contacts among Red Cross Youth in different countries to exchange ideas." Such contacts should help make young people "conscious about . . . intolerance all around the world."

Bulgarian Red Cross (BRC) Youth are also building understanding. The group organizes an international art contest for children with mental and physical disabilities. Many of the children, who are between the ages of 5 and 15, are victims of war. **Art by a Red Cross youth** In 1993, 706 children from Australia, Belarus, Bulgaria, Estonia, Greece, Ireland, Iceland, Italy, Pakistan, Russia, Hungary, the United Kingdom, and Sri

Lanka participated. According to BRC Youth organizer Elena Shadova, the children's art "leads us to their worlds and makes us sensitive to their problems."

Young people who get involved in Red Cross Youth gain many benefits. They learn to be caring individuals who make a practice of helping others. They become more self-confident and aware of their own strengths. They learn to solve problems and take leadership roles—skills that will help them in their careers.

In return, they have much to offer the Red Cross/Red Crescent. Jennie Ågren of Sweden, a young woman in her 20s, described her work with Red Cross Youth as "hard work for a long time." Though she sometimes became discouraged and wanted the Red Cross to be perfect, she knew she could make a difference through RCY. "I feel I have a chance to do something to make this world a little better," she said.

The energy, enthusiasm, and motivation of youth are welcome additions to the Red Cross/Red Crescent. As one chapter leader said, "The future of the Red Cross depends on youth."

What You Can Do

How can you get involved in the Red Cross/Red Crescent? Try any of the following:

1. Call your local Red Cross chapter and ask about local programs for young people. Most chapters offer water safety, first aid, babysitting, and other courses as well as leadership training.

2. Ask your teacher or youth group leader to invite a Red Cross speaker to tell your class or group about international humanitarian law. Your local chapter may supply some materials to make a bulletin board display about the Red Cross.

3. Ask your teacher or youth group leader to show *Light the Darkness*, a 20-minute film that tells the story of the Red Cross/Red Crescent. Contact your local chapter to obtain a copy of the film.

4. Ask your local Red Cross chapter if your youth group or class can participate in a Red Cross project—such as making friendship boxes or school chests. Or choose any project close to home, like taking meals to elderly people in your community.

5. Read a biography of Clara Barton, founder of the American Red Cross. Her dedication and determination will inspire you.

6. Research and write a report on the beginnings of the international Red Cross and Red Crescent movement. Be sure to include Henry Dunant, Clara Barton, and the Geneva Conventions.

Organizations

For more information about Red Cross Youth programs, you can contact one of the following:

Your local Red Cross chapter (listed in your telephone directory)

American Red Cross Division of Youth Involvement
National Office of Volunteers
8111 Gatehouse Road, 2nd Floor
Falls Church, VA 22042
Phone: 703-206-8344
Fax: 703-206-8375

American Red Cross International Services
2025 E Street NW
Washington, D.C. 20006
Phone: (202) 728-6600
Fax: (202) 728-6404

International Federation of Red Cross and Red Crescent Societies
Youth Department
Case Postale 372
CH-1211 Geneva
SWITZERLAND
Phone: (41) 22 730-4222
Fax: (41) 22 733-0395

Index

Acknowledgments

Photographs reproduced with permission of: AP/Wide World Photos, pp. 7 (left), 32, 48; Courtesy of the American Red Cross, pp. 7 (right), 72; Courtesy of the International Federation of Red Cross and Red Crescent Societies, pp. 8, 53, 56, 73, 76; Courtesy of the International Committee of the Red Cross (ICRC)/Boissonnas, pp. 15, 19; Courtesy of ICRC, pp. 16, 20–21; National Archives (#111-SC-39221), 24; Courtesy of the ICRC/Thomas Pizer, p. 25; Courtesy of the ICRC/Didier Bregnard, pp. 40, 42; Courtesy of the ICRC/Alfred Grimm, p. 41; Courtesy of the ICRC/L. de Toledo, p. 45; Courtesy of the ICRC/Paul Grabhorn, p. 49; Bettmann, p. 52; Reuters/Bettmann, p. 59; Courtesy of United Nations High Commissioner for Refugees/P. Moumtzis, p. 57; the *Courier-Journal*, p. 62; Mark Richards, p. 64; Honduran Red Cross Blood Program, p. 67.

Front cover: Courtesy of the ICRC/Thierry Gassmann (*upper left*); Courtesy of the ICRC/Cristina Fedele (*upper right*); Courtesy of the United Nations High Commissioner for Refugees/P. Moumtzis (*lower right*); Courtesy of the ICRC/D. Gignoux (*bottom left*). Back cover: Courtesy of the ICRC.

Illustration: John Erste